RAILWAYS OF THE MIDDLE EAST

THE BRITISH INFLUENCE

Colin Alexander & Alon Siton

AMBERLEY

Front cover: Hedjaz Railway No. 23, RSH No. 7433 of 1952, taken in 1980.

Rear cover: Sudan Government Railways 4-6-2 'Pacific' on the Khartoum passenger train, taken in December 1930.

First published 2020

Amberley Publishing
The Hill, Stroud
Gloucestershire, GL5 4EP

www.amberley-books.com

Copyright © Colin Alexander and
Alon Siton, 2020

The right of Colin Alexander and
Alon Siton to be identified as the Authors of this work has
been asserted in accordance with the Copyrights,
Designs and Patents Act 1988.

ISBN 978 1 4456 8595 3 (print)
ISBN 978 1 4456 8596 0 (ebook)

British Library Cataloguing in Publication Data.
A catalogue record for this book is available from the British Library.

Origination by Amberley Publishing.
Printed in the UK.

Introduction

Like many parts of the world, the Middle East owes much of its railway history to British influence. Britain was heavily involved in the region before the First World War, and the subsequent defeat of the Turkish Ottoman Empire in that same conflict. Britain's presence and influence in the Middle East lasted into the late 1940s, when it could no longer keep the area under control. However, this book is not intended as a piece of academic research into British foreign policy or political history. It is strictly concerned with illustrating some of the history of the Middle East's railways, and aims to shed a romantic, nostalgic light on bygone days in the area, while unavoidably showing some of the effects of conflict in the region.

Principally, the book focuses on four countries with a strong historical connection to Great Britain: Palestine (and later Israel), Egypt, Sudan and Iraq. While Sudan and Egypt are on the African continent, politically and culturally they are affiliated with the Middle East.

Other countries are featured, such as Jordan, whose section of the Hedjaz Railway used several British steam locomotives supplied by North British and Robert Stephenson & Hawthorn. Turkey is included as the demise of its Ottoman Empire is inextricably linked to the railways of the region. Lebanon had its Second World War British military line connecting Beirut and Tripoli along the coast to Haifa. Iran and Syria are also part of the story.

Ever since biblical times, the territory on both sides of the Jordan River (flowing from the Sea of Galilee in the north to the Dead Sea in the south) was considered one complete entity, stretching from the Mediterranean Sea in the west to the deserts of western Iraq. This situation changed dramatically during the First World War, with the British takeover of the whole area and the creation of a new British protectorate, officially named the Emirate of Transjordan.

This book will give a flavour of the golden age of rail travel in the Middle East as a by-product of the growing European political involvement in this part of the world. Starting in the years leading up to 1914, the defeat of the Turkish-Ottoman Empire in the First World War, and right up to the end of the British colonial rule in the post-Second World War era, the book will demonstrate the Middle East's gradual transformation from a distant corner of the Ottoman Empire into a major destination for European travellers, holidaymakers and explorers wishing to discover its important historical and archaeological sites. Central to this new approach was the establishment of a standard gauge railway line between Africa and Asia (specifically between Cairo and Haifa), the introduction of deluxe Compagnie Internationale des Wagons-Lits trains on the international routes, and the construction of a new and modern Mediterranean port in the Bay of Haifa, breathing new life into the Middle East's tourism industry and overall economy.

The post-First World War period of economic growth and peace in the Middle East was, however, short-lived, due to the area's political instability, coupled with Britain's own plans and intentions, the rise of fascism in Europe, and, above all, the outbreak of the Second World War in 1939. For the railways of the Middle East, this was a period of terrorism, sabotaged trains and massive disruption to both military and civilian traffic. During the period of the British Mandate in Palestine, there were countless terror attacks on trains, depots and workshops. It is a sad fact that so much of the region's railway heritage went up in smoke, especially in the 1930s and again in the 1940s, meaning that very little has remained to this day.

Finally, the book will also include photos and reference to the years immediately after the end of the Second World War, showing some of the legacy of British rule and influence in the Middle East from the railways' perspective. This will allow a convenient comparison between the old and the new; that is, the railways of the Middle East under the British and the situation today.

The history of the railways in the Middle East is a complex one, exemplified by the story of the Hedjaz Railway. The construction of this Imperial Ottoman venture over the 820-mile route from Damascus to the holy city of Medina had been a remarkable achievement, beginning in 1901. It was owned by the Turks with equipment supplied by the Germans.

In October 1916, the legendary T. E. Lawrence arrived at Jedda, which was the capital of the Hedjaz before the creation of modern Saudi Arabia. The Hedjaz Railway was of great strategic value to the Turks during wartime. Lawrence realised this, and with the help of his local Arab allies, began his campaign of dynamiting it, putting the railway out of action. Subsequently, the southernmost 523 miles of the route were abandoned.

Following the end of the First World War, the northern section of the Hedjaz Railway was divided between Syria, Palestine and Transjordan. The Syrian section was renamed the Chemin de Fer du Hedjaz, and the Transjordan part of the railway was looked after by Palestine Railways.

Palestine's rail network, under the grand title of Palestine Railways and Operated Lines, was one of the most interesting in the world.

It was operated by a multinational workforce and had been constructed by French, German, Turkish and British engineers. It existed for both religious and military purposes and performed a vital role in the development of that ancient country. It extended from the former territory of Palestine (equating approximately to modern Israel) into Transjordan (modern Jordan) and the Sinai Peninsula of Egypt.

The first railway in Palestine (then part of the Ottoman Empire) was a French-built metre-gauge route linking the port of Jaffa (now part of Tel-Aviv) inland to Jerusalem. This line opened in 1892 and, as well as local traffic, it carried foreign pilgrims to Jerusalem. It was converted to standard gauge by the British Army in the First World War. Arriving from Europe and America, visitors and travellers to the Holy Land crossed the Mediterranean, arriving at the small port of Jaffa, the nearest to Jerusalem, which was around 40 miles inland.

Until the mid-nineteenth century, the best route from Jaffa to Jerusalem was a steep path dating back to Roman times, and there was no reliable transportation. Camels or donkeys carried the tourists' luggage but the modern pilgrims' journey was completed with authenticity, on foot, taking several days in searing summer sun or freezing winter cold. Supplies of food and water were limited, and there was another hazard in the shape of gangs of armed robbers outside Jaffa's city walls. Towards the end of the nineteenth century, horse-drawn carriages were finally introduced on the Jerusalem route, but they still needed two days to complete the journey.

Preliminary attempts made in the 1850s to persuade the Turkish authorities to permit a railway to Jerusalem had failed. The Ottomans refused to grant any land for the proposed project, ostensibly for religious reasons.

It was not until October 1888 that Yosef Navon, an Ottoman Jewish businessman born in Jerusalem, gained official Turkish permission and French finance to build the Jaffa & Jerusalem Railway. In December 1889, the Société du Chemin de fer Ottoman de Jaffa à Jerusalem et Prolongements was formally established in Paris. Construction work commenced in March 1890, under the supervision of Swiss, Polish, Italian and Austrian engineers. The majority of the navvies came from north Africa. The site for Jerusalem station, close to the city, was bought from the Greek Church for the fantastic price of $25,000.

Five 2-6-0 locomotives arrived from the Baldwin Locomotive Works in Philadelphia. Numbered 1–5, they were named *Jaffa, Jerusalem, Ramleh, Lydda* and *El Sejed*. They were joined between 1904 and 1908 by three 0-4-4-0 'Mallet' articulated locomotives from Borsig of Berlin. They were allocated Nos 6–8, with the first two named *Bittir* and *Deir Aban*. A fourth Borsig locomotive, built in 1914, was a casualty of war, being captured at sea and disappearing in Alexandria, Egypt. The railway's ceremonial opening took place on 26 September 1892, beginning with one daily timetabled train through the beautiful Judean hills, taking between four and six hours to cover the tortuous 54-mile journey. It was a slow ride, but it was nevertheless a huge leap forward, and was the safest and most comfortable way to reach Jerusalem.

Further north, in 1905 the Ottoman Government had built a 1,050 mm gauge line through the Jezreel Valley from Haifa to Daraa (or 'Dera'a Junction') in Syria to carry materials needed for the construction of the Hedjaz Railway ('the Pilgrims' Railway'), with which it would eventually connect. It also provided an alternative means of access to the Mediterranean coast to the French-built Beirut–Damascus railway. The Hedjaz Railway headed south through the mountains of the same name to the holy city of Medina in Arabia. In 1920, Palestine Railways took over that part of the HR in British-mandated Palestine, while the sections in French-mandated Syria came under the management of Chemins de Fer du Hedjaz (CFH). Through running continued until June 1946, when a bridge over the Yarmuk River was destroyed by the Jewish Haganah militia. Then, just as Israeli independence was declared in May 1948, what remained of the line was rendered inoperable when Jewish forces destroyed the bridge over the Jordan River at Gesher to thwart the advance of the Arab Legion.

The J&JR, meanwhile, survived for twenty-two years in its original form until the outbreak of the First World War, when it was taken over by combined Turkish and German armies. In 1915, the section from Jaffa to Lydda was dismantled and the rails reused by the Turks to construct a military line to Beersheba (Be'er Sheva), south-west of Jerusalem. The remaining Lydda to Jerusalem section was rebuilt to 1,050 mm gauge, and Lydda became connected to the Hedjaz Railway as well as the route to Beersheba and on to the Egyptian frontier.

As the British advanced from Egypt in 1917, the retreating Austrian forces sabotaged the infrastructure of the railway, destroying major bridges that had to be replaced by temporary trestle structures. The first trainload of British troops reached Jerusalem on 27 December 1917 and soon after the war in the region was over. The Ottoman Empire was defeated and a British Mandate was declared on the territory between the River Jordan and the Mediterranean Sea. During the First World War, despite repeated Turkish attacks, a trunk line was built by the British along the Mediterranean coast, stretching from Egypt to Haifa.

Once the civil administration in the guise of Palestine Railways took over operations from the British Army in October 1920, it assumed responsibility for the rebuilt Jaffa–Jerusalem railway, the Hedjaz Railway, the British-built line from Egypt to Haifa, and Tel-Aviv's suburban services. Palestine's railways attracted scores of wealthy tourists from Europe and North America.

In 1934, Palestine's standard-gauge locomotive fleet consisted mostly of American Baldwin 4-6-0s dating from 1918, handed down by the British military. Another six Baldwins had been converted to 4-6-2 tank engines. There were eleven 0-6-0s, seven of which had come from the London & South Western Railway during the First World War. Heavy freight traffic on the climb to Jerusalem demanded a different solution, and six 2-8-4 tank engines were built by Kitson of Leeds in 1922.

Palestine Railways owned several other British-built locomotives, from Armstrong-Whitworth, Manning Wardle and Nasmyth Wilson, as well as four 120 hp Sentinel Cammell articulated two-car steam railcars, two being for the narrow-gauge section.

The fleet was augmented in 1935 by six handsome P Class 4-6-0 locomotives from the North British Locomotive Co., Glasgow.

As well as new motive power and rolling stock, the railways of Palestine during the period of the British Mandatory Government benefitted from extended routes, modernisation of infrastructure and improved goods handling facilities. It could be said that the new state of Israel reaped these benefits when she was created in 1948.

The General Manager of the Palestine Railways also had a responsibility for the Ports Authority. Under his jurisdiction the port of Haifa was developed considerably in the 1930s to the point where it became one of the most important seaports in the Mediterranean, with facilities for handling crude oil, some of which was piped from Iraq prior to the Arab-Israeli War. Haifa, of course, also had its rail connections into Egypt, Jordan and Syria, and this importance was reflected in the new Haifa Central station, which opened in 1933.

The new regime provided a daily service from Haifa to Kantara on the Suez Canal, featuring Wagons-Lits restaurant and sleeping cars. There were three classes of comfortable accommodation on passenger trains, including sleeping and dining facilities, on services between Haifa and Kantara with attendants, known as *farrashes*, to meet passengers' every need.

At Kantara, the Suez Canal Company provided ferry boats so that passengers could continue their rail journeys to Alexandria or Cairo and beyond.

There followed a period of great upheaval for the railways of Palestine, with politically motivated disturbances and the violent riots of the Arab Revolt from 1936. 1938 was a bad year with forty-four deliberate derailments, the destruction of twenty-seven stations and the sabotage of twenty-one bridges, along with communication and signalling equipment, as well as vital water supplies. A drastic, and certainly unpleasant, solution to the mining of railways was the use of Arab hostages strapped to a single-axle truck on an extended rigid coupling in front of armoured, rail-mounted vehicles – in effect a macabre human minesweeper.

As the Second World War spread from Europe into other parts of the world, rail traffic in Palestine increased dramatically. The main line to Egypt was vital for the supply of the Allied North African Campaign against Rommel's Afrika Korps. Additionally, from the summer of 1941, Palestine Railways provided a supply route for the British invasion of Vichy Syria and Lebanon. This led to the construction of a new railway, north from Haifa, hugging the coast of Haifa Bay and through tunnels into western Lebanon. It was built by a combination of South African and New Zealand engineers. By August 1942 it was able to carry military traffic from Beirut to Egypt. Australian engineers, meanwhile, were working on the Beirut–Tripoli section, which was ready in December 1942. The Haifa–Beirut–Tripoli line was operated by Palestine Railways as far as the Lebanese border where the British Middle East Command took over.

Any hopes that the new military railway would become a permanent peacetime feature were dashed after the war when it was taken over by the Lebanese Government. Rail-borne through traffic between north Africa and eastern Europe via Palestine would remain a dream due to the end of the British Mandate in Palestine and the subsequent Arab-Israeli War.

The declaration of Israeli independence in 1948 led to the severance of all international railway routes. The old Jezreel Valley line from Haifa to Daraa closed completely and the main coastal route was truncated at Nahariyya, near the Lebanese border, and at Ashdod, south of Tel Aviv, on the approach to the Egyptian-ruled Gaza Strip.

Taking over from the erstwhile Palestine Railways, the newly formed Israel State Railways at once launched a fleet and rolling stock modernisation plan, largely relying on West German financial support and equipment under difficult and challenging conditions. Despite severe financial hardship and endless security problems, Israel State Railways managed to build new lines and restore services.

One of the most important was the coastal route from Tel Aviv to Haifa, completed in 1954. A new line to Beersheba was added in 1956, and onwards into the Negev Desert by 1977. The old wooden coaching stock inherited from Palestine Railways was gradually phased out and replaced with new or refurbished vehicles from France, Germany, Yugoslavia and Britain.

American and German diesel locomotives were imported by the dozen but several decades of austerity and stagnation followed. By the millennium, Israel's railways had become neglected, and a much-needed programme of refurbishment and enlargement was begun. By 2011 a thousand kilometres of Israel's railway network was either new or rebuilt and, in 2014, work began on a line from Haifa to Beit She'an, near the border with Jordan, partly following the route of the old Jezreel Valley line. This was intended to eventually link with Jordan.

ISR has a fleet of sixty-two new Bombardier Traxx electric locomotives and double-deck coaches for the new high-speed line from Tel Aviv to Jerusalem. An unprecedented 59.5 million passengers were carried in 2016, compared to 12.7 million in 2000.

The old Jaffa & Jerusalem Railway, having first been absorbed by Palestine Railways, remains active to this day. The new Israel State Railways electric line, however, takes a more direct route through several tunnels and bridges, cutting the journey time from the capital to Tel Aviv to as little as thirty minutes.

Egypt boasted the first railway in Africa when the Khedive of Egypt, Abbas I, engaged Robert Stephenson to build a railway connecting Alexandria to Cairo. The first section opened in 1854 and the 120-mile route necessitated two major bridges across the Nile. The route was then extended to Suez, becoming a vital link in the days before the Suez Canal. A line struck south from Cairo, following the Nile, and reached Luxor, 340 miles away, by 1898.

The First World War brought about a need for a rail link from Egypt into Palestine. The Royal Engineers, under Field Marshal Allenby, began work in 1915 on a standard gauge route from the British Military Headquarters at Kantara, on the Suez Canal, which reached Haifa by 1918. In true British military fashion, Allenby's men did not simply lay a permanent way. As well as the usual railway infrastructure, they also installed water supplies, electricity, telegraph and telephone communications. The demands of the Second World War led to the bridging of the Suez Canal and the through running of trains from Egypt's centres of population across the Sinai into Palestine.

In the glory days of overland travel, Egypt's railways carried large numbers of foreign tourists in the winter season, with special trains meeting European liners at Alexandria. There was also the 'Taurus Express', which brought passengers from London and Paris to Cairo via the Balkans, Turkey, Syria, and Palestine. This involved detraining in Istanbul to cross the Bosphorus into Asia Minor, a road connection from Tripoli (Lebanon) to Haifa, and a crossing of the Suez Canal at Kantara.

The intrepid Europeans would be met from their train at Cairo's impressive station by armies of porters, who would escort their guests to glamorous hotels where they could reflect on the bitter cold they had escaped as they basked on sunny terraces sipping sophisticated cocktails.

The luxurious sleepers and restaurant car of the 'Sunshine Express' would then convey these cosmopolitan travellers south along the Nile to destinations such as Karnak, Luxor and Aswan.

Sudan followed Egypt's lead by opening its first railway in the 1870s. This was intended as a trade route, following the Nile for about 35 miles south from Wadi Halfa near the Egyptian border. The line was commandeered for military use and extended, before abandonment in 1905. It was built to 3 feet 6 inch gauge (also known as Cape Gauge, as used in east and South Africa), reflecting Cecil Rhodes' ambitious but ultimately unrealised hope of a Transafrican trunk route connecting the Cape of Good Hope to Cairo.

Sudan's next railway was another Cape gauge military line built in the 1890s, also starting at Wadi Halfa but heading south-east over 200 miles to Abu Hamad. It eventually reached Atbarah (which would become Sudan's 'railway city') and, following General Kitchener's defeat of the Mahdi, Khartoum was reached by 1899. The line was converted from military to civilian traffic and formed the basis of today's Sudanese railway.

A narrow-gauge network, the Gezira Light Railway, evolved from the 1920s for the construction of canals, expanding into a system serving agricultural communities at the confluence of the Blue and White Nile Rivers near Khartoum.

The fortunes of Sudan's railways declined sharply in the late 1960s and early 1970s, and the ensuing civil war severed complete sections of the network. Recent efforts to restore services and modernise infrastructure have been hampered by continuing civil unrest.

In a parallel with Israel, Sudan's rail network had no international connections. This changed in 2011 with the creation of the Republic of South Sudan and a new international border which crossed the Khartoum to Wau railway between Babanusa and Aweil. A 2009 proposal for a standard gauge link from Wadi Halfa connecting with Egyptian Railways at Aswan is yet to be realised. Meanwhile, in 2017, a feasibility study was authorised for an ambitious 2,000-mile standard gauge route linking Port Sudan on the Red Sea with N'Djamena, the capital of Chad, in the heart of the African continent.

The first railway in Iraq was of standard gauge and opened in 1914, connecting Baghdad with the ancient city of Samarra, 75 miles to the north. This was part of the grand Ottoman Baghdad Railway scheme to link the Iraqi capital with Istanbul and thence Berlin. Iraq's railways spread to the main areas of population, especially in the valleys of Mesopotamia, and mostly built at metre gauge. Some of these were converted to standard gauge in the 1980s, while the rest were abandoned. A new line from Baghdad to the Syrian border at Hsaiba was completed in 1983, and another connecting Haditha to Kirkuk opened in 1987.

Like many other railways of the Middle East, by the beginning of the twenty-first century, Iraq's network was run down, the Gulf War of the 1990s having taken its toll. Still, more than a thousand miles of the system remained, including the original Baghdad Railway to Turkey via Syria.

The Second Gulf War, beginning in 2003, devastated what was left and peacetime recovery has been slow. By 2012, Baghdad's commuter routes, as well as long distance trains from the capital to Al-Basrah, Fallujah and Mosul, were back in service. The latter city was cut off again in 2014 after a terrorist takeover. Following liberation in 2017 it may be some time before restoration of this vital rail link is complete.

The first railway line in Jordan was the aforementioned Hedjaz Railway, opened in 1908 between the Syrian capital, Damascus, and Medina in Saudi Arabia. The line's recent history has been blighted by the Syrian conflict, and cross-border traffic has stopped.

Regular services operate between Jordan's capital, Amman, and Al-Mafraq, 40 miles north-east, and steam haulage is occasionally employed.

The Aqaba Railway connects phosphate mines in southern Jordan to the port of Al-Aqabah on the eastern arm of the Red Sea. Its route is that of the old Hedjaz Railway, and there is a long-term aim for this to form part of a modern national Jordanian rail system incorporating the rebuilt Hedjaz Railway with new international links.

The first railway in what is now Turkey, then the Ottoman Empire, opened in 1858 from Alsancak in the far west of Asia Minor, eventually forming part of the main line to Aydin.

Surprisingly, it was another thirty years before Constantinople (now Istanbul), on the European side of the Bosphorus, got its first railway through Greece and the Balkans to the rest of Europe. This famously became the eastern section of the route of the Orient Express from Paris.

The birth of the new republic of Turkey in 1927 also saw the creation of Turkish State Railways (TCDD).

A long-projected link with Iran opened in 1971 and more significantly a new tunnel under the Bosphorus connects the European and Asian parts of Turkey by rail.

A new international route from Turkey into Georgia opened in 2017, providing an alternative route to Azerbaijan and the oil terminals on the Caspian Sea.

Lebanon has been under French influence since the First World War and the May 1916 signing of the Sykes-Picot Agreement. This resulted in the once-great Ottoman Empire being carved up between Great Britain, France and, to a lesser extent, Russia. In the Second World War Lebanon became, by default, part of Vichy France, although European politics had little influence in Beirut.

The first railway in what is now Lebanon opened in 1895 when it was part of the Ottoman Empire. It connected the major port of Beirut to Damascus, and like several others in the region it was built to the gauge of 1,050 mm. It passed through the magnificent scenery of the Lebanese Alps.

A junction of sorts was formed in 1906 at Riyaq (also known as 'Rayaq') from which a line was constructed to Aleppo in northern Syria. This was a standard gauge line, so goods and passengers had to be trans-shipped. In 1911 another branch was opened from Homs, now over the border in Syria, to the Lebanese port of Tripoli (Ṭarābulus).

As mentioned above, during the Second World War Allied forces extended the Tripoli line down the coast, via Beirut, to Palestine, but the dream of forming a through route from Turkey to North Africa was dashed as the Lebanese section was purchased by the government. Its southern terminus became Naqoura, just a couple of miles north of the modern border with Israel.

The Lebanese rail network continued in this state until the civil war of the 1970s, which virtually wiped out its infrastructure. There have been various proposals to reinstate all or part of the Lebanese rail system, but to date no progress has been made.

When Iran was still known as Persia, its first railway opened in 1888 between Tehran and the holy shrine of Shah-Abdol-Azim at Rey. This was a short, narrow gauge line intended for pilgrims, but later branch lines were added serving quarries.

Persia had to wait until 1914 for her first major railway, a 90-mile standard gauge line connecting the northern outpost of Tabriz to Jolfa, on the border with present-day Azerbaijan (then part of Russia). As Persia became Iran in 1935 her total railway mileage amounted to less than 500.

The construction of the Trans-Iranian Railway from Bandar-e Torkeman, on the Caspian Sea, south to Bandar-e Shahpur, on the Persian Gulf, during the Second World War trebled this figure in one go. Today, the Islamic Republic of Iran Railways boasts a standard gauge network of over 6,000 miles, with more planned. In 1977 it was physically connected to the west at the Turkish border, and in 1993 a line was opened to Bandar-e Abbas on the Strait of Hormuz. Another international connection was established in 1996 with a line linking Mashad to Sarakhs on the border with Turkmenistan, part of the so-called 'Silk Road Railway' into landlocked Central Asia.

There are also schemes in progress to connect Iran with neighbouring Iraq and Afghanistan. It can be seen, therefore, that the Middle East railway scene continues to be in a state of constant flux, with new international connections being made.

I must acknowledge the contribution of my co-author, Alon Siton, whose photographic collection forms the basis for the book, and without whose patience, encouragement and local knowledge it would not have been possible.

This map from *The Illustrated London News* of 26 November 1910 shows the route of the proposed London to Bombay railway, which would also have connected to Russia. The journey to India was expected to take up to eight days over a total distance of 5,554 miles via Berlin, Baku and Baluchistan. (Alon Siton Collection)

This topographical map of the Middle East dates from 1920 and shows the main British and Turkish rail routes connecting Egypt with Palestine, Lebanon, Syria, Jordan and Arabia (a section that was sabotaged during the First World War and subsequently abandoned). The Suez Canal connects the Mediterranean to the Gulf of Suez and the Red Sea. (Alon Siton Collection)

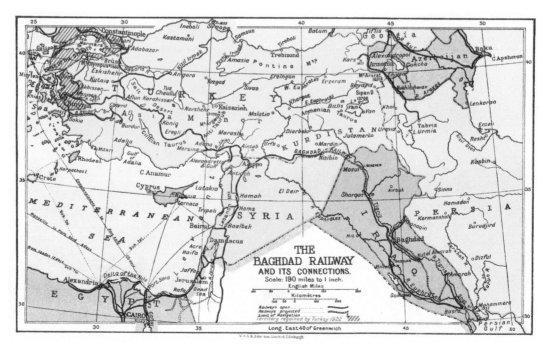

A coloured map of 1922, showing the route of the Baghdad Railway between Turkey and Iraq, with connections at Aleppo Junction and Damascus to Jerusalem, Cairo and on to Sudan and elsewhere in Africa. Note the gap (shown as Projected Railway) between Syria and Iraq, necessitating the use of a special bus for the long ride across the desert. (Alon Siton Collection)

Palestine/Israel

The French-built metre gauge Jaffa & Jerusalem Railway was the first in Palestine, opening in 1892. It was operated by five 2-6-0 locomotives supplied by Baldwin of Pennsylvania, and later three Borsig Mallet locomotives. First of the Baldwins, No. 1 *Jaffa*, is seen here at Jerusalem station in 1904. (Alon Siton Collection)

This historic photograph shows a ceremony involving No. 1 *Jaffa*, decorated with Ottoman flags. The rails in the foreground do not appear to be spiked to the sleepers yet. The image was probably taken in 1892 and shows a small crowd of exotically dressed colonial and native spectators gathered for the event. The bearded gentleman to the left of the locomotive, in a black top hat and white trousers, is William H. Crawford from Baldwin, who was sent to Palestine to supervise the erection of the locomotives. (Alon Siton Collection)

A typical view of the J&JR station at Jerusalem looking quite new, so probably taken in the 1890s. The mixed train of goods and passenger vehicles from Jaffa is headed by Baldwin 2-6-0 No. 4 *Lydda*. The dignified station building still exists in Jerusalem and is now used as a commercial centre. (Alon Siton Collection)

The Jaffa & Jerusalem Railway built a short extension into the Mediterranean Sea at the port of Jaffa. The small crane on the end of the wooden jetty would allow trans-shipment of goods. Note the ships anchored in the 'roadstead' out at sea. (Alon Siton Collection)

In contrast to Jaffa's Mediterranean shores, this is Dir A-Ban station on the J&JR. The Judean hills form the backdrop to this idyllic, panoramic pre-First World War photo. One of the five Baldwin 2-6-0s and a baggage van are at the head of this passenger train. (Alon Siton Collection)

Additional motive power arrived on the Jaffa & Jerusalem Railway when the Baldwin 'Moguls' were joined by three 0-4-4-0 'Mallet' locomotives built by Borsig of Berlin. This rare glass slide shows one of the trio at Jerusalem station, with a mixed train for Jaffa, in 1910. A fourth member of the class was captured by the Royal Navy in transit during the First World War and never delivered. Partly visible in the background is the Montefiore Windmill and, beyond that, Jerusalem's new city. (Alon Siton Collection)

The Hedjaz Railway built a junction station at Na'an, where the Turkish line to Beersheba branched off from the Damascus-Haifa main line. Close inspection of this panoramic view, taken around the time of the First World War, reveals several Jaffa & Jerusalem Railway passenger coaches, a single Hedjaz Railway freight wagon and, to the left, what appears to be a sister engine of the Krauss 0-6-0T (seen on page 37) in the museum at Haifa. (Alon Siton Collection)

Palestine Military Railways employed several former London & South Western Railway Adams 0-6-0s. This fascinating First World War photo shows one hauling the region's first British ambulance train along the line from Jaffa to Jerusalem, somewhere in the Judean hills. The route had been converted to standard gauge during the First World War. (Israel Railways Museum)

The Hedjaz Railway owned three 2-6-2T locomotives built by La Meuse of Liege, Belgium, in 1914, works Nos 2419–2421. In this 1918 view of Jerusalem station, British officers are considering how to extract No. 2420 from the turntable well. Note the station building and water tower in the background. (Israel Railways Museum)

By 1918 four of the J&JR Baldwin 2-6-0s had been destroyed by the retreating Turks, leaving only No. 3 *Ramleh* intact. Those same Turkish troops were responsible for pushing No. 2420 into the turntable well (see above) from which she has now been successfully extricated by the little Baldwin. (Ron Garraway, courtesy of Israel Railways Museum)

La Meuse also built three 0-10-0T locomotives in 1914. They were captured by the British en route from Belgium to a Turkish customer, and sent to Palestine to work on the Hedjaz Railway. The original customer was never compensated for the loss. They became HR Nos 2432, 2435 and 2436, the same as their works numbers. One of these, No. 2435, stands next to 2-8-0T No. 71, converted from a 2-8-0 tender locomotive built by Jung of Germany in 1907. The setting is Haifa station in 1919, with the picturesque town clearly visible beyond. (Israel Railways Museum)

For the steep gradients on the route from Jaffa to Jerusalem, in 1922 Palestine Railways obtained six new 2-8-4 tank locomotives from Kitson of Leeds, England. This official portrait shows PR No. 1. They were designated Class K, with 4-foot-diameter drivers to cope with heavy traffic on mountain gradients, but were prone to derailment. (Alon Siton Collection)

The Birmingham Railway Carriage & Wagon Co. was founded in the 1850s and enjoyed an international reputation for its vehicles. Palestine Railways saloon No. 98 was built there in 1922 and is now preserved at the Israel Railways Museum, Haifa. Her illustrious passengers have included Emperor Haile Selassie of Ethiopia, Queen Elizabeth of Belgium and Sir Winston Churchill. She is reported to have ventured as far north as Istanbul, carrying the last Palestine Railways CEO, Arthur Kirby, to the International Railway Conference that was held there in 1946. (Paul Cotterell, courtesy of Israel Railways Museum)

This wonderful panoramic view of downtown Haifa and the Mediterranean Sea was taken from Mount Carmel in 1934. Three Palestine Railways passenger coaches and several goods wagons are in the waterfront sidings. A battleship, thought to be HMS *Barham*, is sailing out of Haifa Bay into the open sea, while a light cruiser of either C or D Class is moored inside the breakwater. Note the Turkish clock tower in the extreme bottom left – a remnant of pre-First World War Ottoman rule in the Middle East. (Alon Siton Collection)

A most iconic Palestine Railways photo, dating from the glamorous, glory days of the 1930s. This is the splendid sight of Haifa East station and the Cairo Express, which includes Wagons Lits vehicles about to depart on the long journey across the Sinai Desert to Africa. Baldwin Class H 4-6-0 steam locomotive No. 892 is in charge of this prestigious international service. (Israel Railways Museum)

Palestine Railways Class H2 4-6-2T No. 8 brings a special train carrying Crown Prince Faisal of Saudi Arabia into Jerusalem station on an official visit in 1935. The locomotive was originally one of the fifty Baldwin H Class 4-6-0s for the Palestine Military Railway in 1918, but limited turntable facilities led to six of them being sent, in 1926, to Armstrong Whitworth in Newcastle for rebuilding as tank locomotives. (Alon Siton Collection)

Seen in her later years under the ownership of Israel Railways, ex-Palestine Railways P Class 4-6-0 No. 60 is turned at Haifa. Six of these handsome mixed traffic locomotives were built by the North British Locomotive Company of Glasgow in 1935, as works Nos 24219–24224. (Alon Siton Collection)

Another British export for Palestine Railways was this third-class coach, No. 338, built at the Gloucester Railway Carriage & Wagon Co. in 1935. It is seen being unloaded from a Christen-Smith ship at the port of Haifa. Another two new coaches are visible on the dockside beyond. Moored behind and overshadowing the ship is another symbol of European tourism, the Italian luxury liner SS *Roma*, on a Mediterranean cruise. (Israel Railways Museum)

An interesting view of the Turkish-built station at Haifa in the 1930s, showing passengers getting off a boat to board a Palestine Railways train. Rising over the station building is Mount Carmel, and the large Hedjaz Railway building on the left now serves a new role as the main archive of the Israel Railways Museum. (Alon Siton Collection)

This 1936 photo shows British soldiers changing trains after an act of sabotage made the line impassable near Lydda Junction. Terrorists had torn up several hundred yards of the railway, so a collective fine of £5,000 was imposed on the population of Lydda. When the fine was not paid, tanks and armoured cars were sent in to enforce payment. (Alon Siton Collection)

Another example of part of the horrific and sustained terror campaign against Palestine Railways, this freight train was sabotaged on the main line from Haifa to Lydda Junction in August 1936. In another incident, a British military pay train was sabotaged and £35,000 was taken. (Alon Siton Collection)

Extensive damage was caused to this Palestine Railways train in a terror attack in October 1938, causing the derailment and overturning of two Baldwin 4-6-0 locomotives. This inevitably caused major disruption on the main line between Haifa and Lydda Junction. (Alon Siton Collection)

A Palestine Railways P Class 4-6-0 with a passenger train (possibly the Haifa–Cairo Express) at Lydda Junction in 1938, preceded by a rail-mounted armoured car. The regular use of such military escorts became necessary due to multiple attacks on the railway lines in Palestine at the time. Arab hostages were strapped into the seats over the forward axle as a deterrent to mine-laying saboteurs. (Alon Siton Collection)

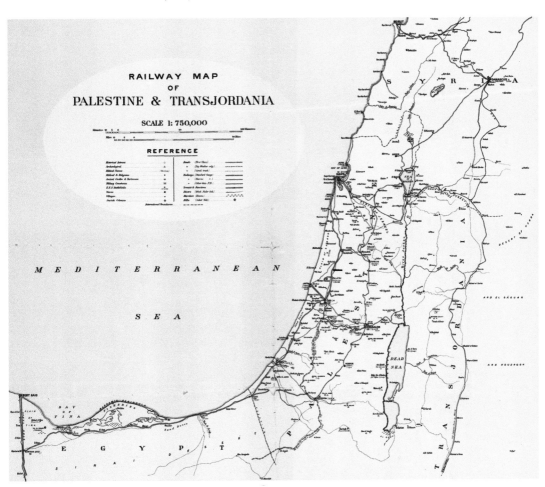

A pre-Second World War British map of Palestine and 'Transjordania', showing the Palestine Railways network as well as the Hedjaz Railway on both sides of the Jordan River. Moreover, it shows British Expeditionary Force battlefields. Note the still-missing Haifa, Beirut & Tripoli Railway, which extended up the coast from 1942 and was intended to reach Turkey. Kantara East, on the Suez Canal in Egypt, is at the south-west corner of the map. (Alon Siton Collection)

The unfortunate aftermath of an altercation between a Palestine Railways train and a Volvo M653F bus operated by Egged, the public transport company, can be seen in this 1939 photograph. Twenty-nine bus passengers were killed in the violent collision near the city of Ramleh. (Alon Siton Collection)

182 Railway Operating Company was a specialised division of the Royal Engineers. Among the motive power at their disposal was this outside-cylindered 0-6-0T. She was one of ten Class Ns obtained by Palestine Railways from 1934, for shunting duties, from Nasmyth, Wilson of Manchester. Other men from 182 ROC were deployed on diesel locomotives operating the line from Kantara to El Shatt, near Suez. (Israel Railways Museum)

Jenin, in the Samaria region of Palestine, is the likely location for this summer 1941 photograph of a train carrying Australian Royal Engineers, who were engaged in reconditioning the former Turkish Hedjaz Railway, from Tul Karm to Afula Junction. The motive power is No. 2432, one of the La Meuse 0-10-0T locomotives. A New Zealand RE company used the line in connection with military operations in Syria. It then was closed until October 1944, when Palestine Railways began operating freight trains. (Alon Siton Collection)

This fascinating view of the British-built Second World War railway line from Haifa to Beirut and Tripoli in Lebanon shows its proximity to the Mediterranean at Rosh Hanikra. The line was inaugurated in 1942, to be abandoned only five years later in 1947. The railway was dismantled and a local road was built on its trackbed. (Alon Siton Collection)

Many thousands of Jewish refugees escaped the Nazis in Europe for Palestine. They included the so-called 'Tehran children', who made the tortuous journey from Poland via Iran, Pakistan and the Red Sea to Suez. This poignant photograph shows an Egyptian State Railways train carrying fortunate escapees being welcomed as it enters Hadera, between Haifa and Tel Aviv, on 18 February 1943. (Alon Siton Collection)

Among the possessions of a soldier serving in the Royal Engineers in the North Africa campaign was this military-issue Palestine Railways third-class Haifa–Cairo train ticket, dated 21 May 1943. This is yet another illustration of the influence of the British on the world's railways, being of the standard Edmondson type of ticket introduced in England in the 1840s. (Alon Siton Collection)

As well as the famous Robinson 2-8-0s, the wartime Railway Operating Division used ex-London & South Western Railway 0-6-0s, of which twenty-nine examples were inherited by Palestine Railways. This is former L&SWR No. 508, built by Neilson in Glasgow in 1885, at Haifa-Kishon Workshops on 22 January 1945. She had been withdrawn from service in 1937. (Alon Siton Collection)

Another of the North British mixed traffic 4-6-0s of Class P, No. 65, is seen at Lydda Junction on 25 January 1945. The six members of the class lasted until 1960, but unfortunately nothing more than two of the bogie tenders survive in preservation. (Alon Siton Collection)

At first glance, one could be forgiven for thinking this photograph was taken somewhere on British Railways' London Midland region in the 1950s. It is, in fact, another view of Lydda Junction in March 1945, with Stanier 8F 2-8-0 No. 70305 in attendance. She was built by North British in Glasgow, in 1940, as works No. 24605, one of many supplied to the War Department. (Alon Siton Collection)

A marvellous view of Palestine Railways' Haifa East station in 1945, with the Cairo train at the platform. The old Hedjaz Railway workshops are clearly seen to the left, with a steam locomotive outside the left entrance. This building now provides a safe home for the Israel Railways Museum's historical rolling stock collection. (Alon Siton Collection)

Another Stanier 8F 2-8-0, No. 70391, at Haifa in September 1950. She was originally delivered to the War Department as No. 391, first becoming Iranian Railways No. 41.145 before passing into the stock of Israel Railways. She was built by North British Locomotive Co. in Glasgow in 1941 as works No. 24699. (Alon Siton Collection)

By the traverser at Haifa Kishon are the remains of a steam crane and some ex-WD 8Fs. In-between is a German 550 D14 diesel hydraulic, the Third Reich locomotive that helped the Allies. Originally No. 11118, she was built by Berliner Maschinenbau and sent to Africa to assist with Rommel's military campaign. She was captured by the British in 1943 and sent to Haifa, and as WD No. 70246 was used on the military line to Lebanon. After the war she was earmarked for potential use in Israel but remained out of service and was scrapped in 1958. (Alon Siton Collection)

Ex-Palestine Railways Baldwin 4-6-0 No. 883, Stanier 8F 2-8-0 No. 70503 (North British 24711 of 1941), and another 8F were used for bridge testing late in 1954. The Yarkon River bridge is on the then recently completed main line between Haifa and Tel Aviv. Officially inaugurated on 4 November 1954, the line provided a direct link between the two cities along the new coastal route. The surrounding eucalyptus trees and rich vegetation were once a common sight in this area. (Israel Railways Museum)

A border checkpoint with Israeli military policemen inspecting the line as it crosses from the Egyptian-occupied Gaza Strip into Israel. A section of the line was destroyed in an Arab raid on 3 December 1957. Originally built in the First World War in conjunction with the British military advance from Egypt, the main line from Haifa to Cairo was a key international route for nearly twenty years. This important service ceased after the end of the British Mandate in Palestine and the subsequent political unrest in the Middle East. No trains pass here today, in either direction. (Alon Siton Collection)

This classic 1950s scene in Israel depicts a new SAFB (Société Anglo-Franco-Belge/General Motors) diesel locomotive pulling into Na'an station, south of Tel Aviv, with a passenger service. The leading coach was built by Orenstein & Koppel of Berlin in 1953. These vehicles were wide, spacious and comfortable. Note the original British-built mechanical lower-quadrant semaphore signals still in use. (Paul Cotterell/Israel Railways Museum)

An official Israel Railways colour photo of the neat new railway station at Beersheba in the 1950s, with SAFB diesel locomotive No. 102, built in 1952, at the head of a passenger train from Tel Aviv. The station buffet is open for business. (Israel Railways Museum)

קרון מזנון

A member of the train crew poses in the vestibule of Israel (ex-Palestine) Railways buffet car No. 504 sometime in the 1950s. The vehicle was the first of a pair built by the Metropolitan Carriage & Wagon Co. of Birmingham, each seating eighty third-class passengers. (Alon Siton Collection)

ISRAEL

Benno Ruthenberg's 1959 colour poster of an Israel State Railways diesel train on the way to Jerusalem. This is the only known colour photograph of one of the Maschinenfabrik Esslingen diesel-multiple-unit trains in the original blue livery with 'vee' whiskers on the front. (Alon Siton Collection)

In the Six Day War of 1967, Israel captured several Egyptian diesel locomotives including three Class G16 Co-Cos, Nos 3304, 3329 and 3361. They were absorbed into Israel Railways stock as Nos 301–303, later 161–163. This is one of the trio departing El Arish station, on the north coast of Sinai, for the long run to Haifa. She is adorned with four Israeli flags and a large ISR logo between the buffers, above which is proudly displayed the emblem of the State of Israel, consisting of the menorah and olive branches. (Alon Siton Collection)

A wonderful view of the exterior of Jerusalem railway station in 1967. Note the huge '20' on the right and the more understated '75' on the white banner on the left. They commemorate, respectively, twenty years since the establishment of the State of Israel and the seventy-fifth anniversary of the first railway line in the Holy Land, the Jaffa & Jerusalem Railway. (Alon Siton Collection)

This is Haifa shed in 1968 with one of Israel Railways' ex-Egyptian State Railways General Motors (EMD) Co-Co Class G16 diesel locomotives, No. 303. The former ESR No. 3361 is preserved at the Israel Railway Museum in Haifa. (Israel Railways Museum)

A colourful ISR passenger train, with General Motors diesel locomotive No. 603 and a rake of six ex-British Rail coaches during their inaugural run in Israel, at Haifa Bat-Galim on 28 April 1977. A total of eight refurbished Mk IIc coaches, dating from 1969, were purchased by Israel Railways and, despite having air-conditioning fitted in 1989, they were withdrawn by around 1997. (Israel Railways Museum)

This nocturnal scene depicts another ex-Egyptian diesel in Israel. This is Class G12 Bo-Bo No. 129 at Haifa diesel depot in the 1980s. Israel imported twenty-three of these locomotives from GM from 1954 and added to its fleet by capturing another four from Egypt during the Six Day War. Sister loco No. 130 was a casualty of the same war, and 106 was a sabotage victim. Happily, No. 107 is preserved in the museum at Haifa East. (Paul Cotterell/Israel Railways Museum)

A pleasing view of Haifa East railway station, taken in September 2014, shows some of the rolling stock collection of the adjacent Israel Railways Museum, housed in the former engine shed. Taking centre stage among the open-air exhibits is an impressive steam crane, built by Cowans-Sheldon of Carlisle. (Alon Siton Collection)

A panoramic aerial view of the beautiful Mediterranean coastline at Rosh Hanikra, north of Haifa Bay and close to the Lebanese border, in 2015. The famous white cliff, known as the Ladder of Tyre, can be seen in the distance. From 1942 to 1947, this was the location of the Haifa, Beirut & Tripoli Railway's main line. Little remains of the abandoned railway today but its route can be traced to the right of the small road bridge and along the local road leading to the north. (Alon Siton Collection)

This 2016 photograph was taken from the Israeli side of the border looking into Jordan, with its military post on the hill. The Jisr el Mujamie bridge was the lowest point on any railway in the world at 845 feet below sea level. It carried the Turkish-German Hedjaz Railway's main line from Haifa to Damascus. It was completed in 1904 and was irreparably damaged in 1948, during an Israeli military operation to keep advancing Arab forces away from the new State of Israel. Even the river is no more, as hardly any water is allowed to flow from the Sea of Galilee into the Dead Sea today. (Alon Siton Collection)

The Hedjaz Railway's Beersheba station is the incongruous new home of Stanier 8F 2-8-0 North British works No. 24641 of 1940. She was delivered as LMSR No. 8267, becoming War Department No. 341 and, after the war, was absorbed into Turkish State Railways stock as TCDD No. 45166. She was recovered from Sivas, Turkey, in 2010, by the Churchill 8F Trust and brought to Israel in 2012. She is displayed in the spirit of a popular Israeli song from the 1950s, commonly known as 'The Locomotive's Song', about the last voyage of sister engine No. 70414 (whose identity she now wears) from Beersheba to the scrapyard in Haifa, marking the end of the steam era in the Holy Land. (Alon Siton Collection)

Inside the Israel Railways Museum at Haifa East, on 7 November 2018, we see the only steam locomotive in the collection. This is Hedjaz Railway 0-6-0T No. 10, built by Krauss of Linz, Austria, in 1902 as works No. 4723. Since this photograph was taken, she has been turned through 180°. This was achieved, despite her seized wheels, by greasing the rails, sliding her outside, then lifting and turning with a large crane and a crew of able-bodied men. Imagine this little machine in her heyday, climbing the gradient to Damascus! (Alon Siton Collection)

Egypt

Egypt led the way with the first railway in the Ottoman Empire, Africa and the Middle East, opening in 1854 between Alexandria and Kafr el-Zayyat on the River Nile. At first, the railway crossed the Nile using an 80-foot train ferry. Disaster struck on 15 May 1858, when human error caused a train carrying Prince Ahmad Rifaat Pasha to run off the ferry and into the river where the royal heir drowned. Robert Stephenson replaced the ferry with a tubular viaduct incorporating one of the longest swing bridge sections built, being over 150 feet long. (Alon Siton Collection).

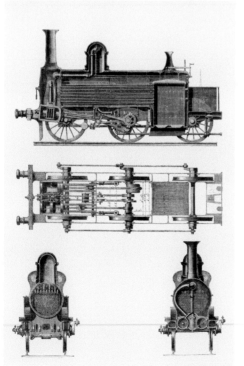

This beautiful engineering drawing was published in *The Engineer* magazine in 1858. It shows an 0-6-0 locomotive built by Sharp, Stewart & Co. at the Atlas Works in Manchester for the Pasha of Egypt. For a humble goods engine she was lavishly decorated, typifying the coming together of Victorian engineering efficiency and aesthetic beauty. (Alon Siton Collection)

Three of these distinctive 2-2-4 locomotives were built in the late 1850s and early 1860s by Robert Stephenson & Co. in Newcastle for the Viceroy of Egypt, each with a luxurious saloon mounted behind the footplate. According to a contemporary issue of the *Newcastle Courant*, 'The exterior of the train is decorated with arabesque designs of black, white and gold, in the first style of art, from the designs of Mr Digby Wyatt'. One of them, known as the Pasha's train, can be admired today in the railway museum in Cairo. (Alon Siton Collection)

John Fowler & Co. of Leeds was known for its agricultural steam engines, but the firm also built railway locomotives. Most of these were for domestic industrial use but some were for the export market. One of these was Egyptian State Railways 2-4-0T No. 43 *Minieh*, built in 1872, of which this is the only known photograph. Note her unusual outside-framed front pony-truck and American-style spark-arresting chimney. (ETH Zürich)

This wonderful vintage Zangaki Brothers photograph shows a passenger train at Suez in 1875. At this time the canal of that name had been open for six years and several large vessels can be seen in the distance. The train consists of an elegant 2-4-0ST with a livestock van and three third-class wooden passenger cars. (Alon Siton Collection)

My favourite photograph in the book, taken at Alexandria around 1882, shows a British Naval Brigade armoured train powered by an outside-framed 0-6-0. The crew are from HMS *Hecla*, which was a torpedo ship involved in the bombardment of Alexandria in July of that year. (Alon Siton Collection)

An official portrait of a new 2-2-2 locomotive, No. 17, for the Egyptian State Railways built by Kitson of Hunslet, Leeds, in 1889. She was one of six such locomotives, works Nos 3166–3171, and numbered 16–21 in Egypt. Mostly withdrawn by 1926, No. 19 survived long enough to become ESR No. 500, while her sisters were scrapped. (ETH Zürich)

Another charming Zangaki Brothers photograph of Suez station, this time taken in 1890. It shows an elegant Robert Stephenson & Co. long-boiler outside-cylinder, inside-framed 4-2-0, built in Newcastle around 1855. (Alon Siton Collection)

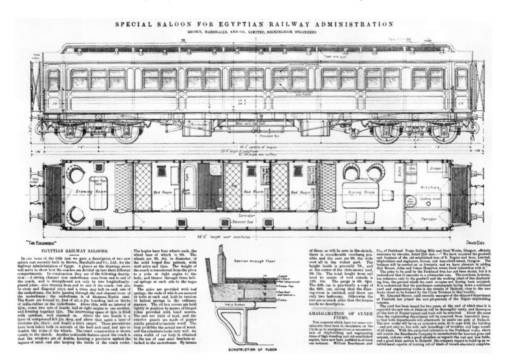

SPECIAL SALOON FOR EGYPTIAN RAILWAY ADMINISTRATION
BROWN, MARSHALLS, AND CO. LIMITED, BIRMINGHAM, ENGINEERS

An engineering drawing of a Special Saloon coach for the Egyptian Railway Administration, built by Brown, Marshalls & Co. of Birmingham in 1900. This illustration appeared in a contemporary issue of *The Engineer*. The coach was one of a pair featuring sleeping and dining accommodation. (Alon Siton Collection)

An impressive sight at Alexandria is this 'De Glehn' 4-4-2, built by Société Française de Constructions Mécaniques in 1905. Egyptian State Railways had ten such locomotives, numbered 667–676. A trio of similar French engines ran on the Great Western Railway. One of the gentlemen in the photo is John Thomas Hall (driver) who left England on Christmas Eve 1894, en route for Wadi Halfa and the Sudan war. (Alon Siton collection)

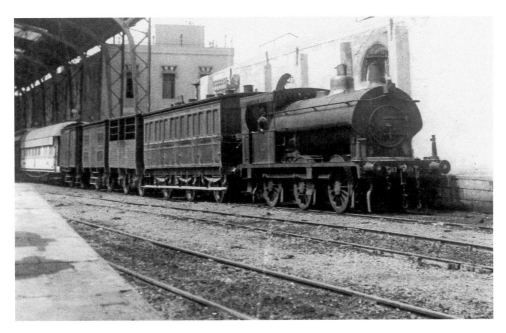

Egyptian State Railways 0-6-0ST No. 517 was built by Franco-Belge in 1905 as works No. 1291. This undated photo, presumably at Cairo, shows her shunting a train of freight and passenger stock. The leading six-wheel coach was built in 1889 by Oldbury Carriage Works in Birmingham. It is coupled to a livestock truck, then follows a perishables van and what appears to be a postal van. The white vehicle is a Wagons Lits dining car, behind which is a clerestory-roofed coach. (Alon Siton Collection)

This handsome outside-framed 4-4-0 was Egyptian State Railways No. 224, one of fifteen such locomotives built for service in Egypt by the North British Locomotive Co. in Glasgow in 1905–06. Their works numbers were NBL 16882–16896. (Alon Siton Collection)

Another Egyptian State Railways 4-4-0 locomotive, possibly from the same batch as that above, is in charge of a passenger train at Tanta station, between Alexandria and Cairo, in the 1910s. Notice the locomotive crewman standing on the cowcatcher and inspecting between the frames. (Alon Siton Collection)

Somewhere in the Sinai desert between Egypt and Palestine during the First World War, the rear of a makeshift British military train is seen in this vintage photograph. To say that the troops' accommodation is rudimentary is an understatement. Note the six-wheeled Egyptian brake van at the tail. (Alon Siton Collection)

This amazing photograph shows the swing bridge over the Suez Canal, at Kantara, in 1917. A freight train hauled by an unidentified 0-6-0ST is crossing the dead-straight waterway. The bridge seems to have been dismantled after the First World War and replaced by a ferry. (Alon Siton Collection)

The British military advance from Egypt into Palestine during the First World War resulted in the taking of several locomotives as 'spoils of war'. This narrow gauge 0-10-0T, built by Belgian firm La Meuse in 1914, is at Kantara, a considerable distance from the Hedjaz, the railway which ordered her. The captured La Meuse locomotives were overhauled and put to work by the British in Palestine. (Israel Railways Museum)

'Visit Egypt by train' is a beautiful example of an Egyptian State Railways advertisement dating from 1925. The stylised Nefertiti-like figure and vivid blue/gold colour scheme are clearly designed to lure would-be amateur Egyptologists to North Africa by train. (Alon Siton Collection)

Intrepid travellers tempted to Africa by such posters might be hauled by an Egyptian State Railways 4-4-2 such as No. 35, seen here. Originally numbered 769, No. 35 was built by North British Locomotive Co. in Glasgow in 1925, works No. 23318. The thirty-five 'Atlantics' built by NBL were joined by similar locomotives built in France, Germany and the USA, all to the specification of J. Langton, the chief mechanical engineer of the Egyptian State Railways. (Alon Siton Collection)

This busy scene depicts an important day in the history of Egyptian State Railways: the official opening of the upgraded standard gauge line from Luxor to Aswan in 1926. In attendance are several dignitaries including Adli Yakn Pasha, on the right, and a heavy military presence. (Alon Siton Collection)

It was not just the British who supplied handsome outside-framed 4-4-0 locomotives to Egypt. This immaculate example, No. 331, seen at Suez station in 1928, was built by Henschel of Kassel, Germany, in 1906. She is of similar design to her North British-built contemporary. (Alon Siton Collection)

Not the Middle East, but the East of England, where a two-car steam railcar is seen on a test run at the now-closed station at Woodhall Junction. She was built in 1928 by the Clayton Carriage & Wagon Co. in nearby Lincoln. They entered service as Egyptian State Railways Nos 5000–5004, and 5100. (Alon Siton Collection)

Lord Armstrong of Cragside, Northumberland, was one of the great Victorian innovators and philanthropists. The vast Armstrong Whitworth works by the Tyne at Elswick manufactured hydraulic machinery, guns, ships, rail and road vehicles, and aircraft. Among the locomotives built there was a batch of twenty Class 545 2-6-0s in 1928 for Egyptian State Railways, of which No. 603 is seen here. (Alon Siton Collection)

Not all Egyptian rolling stock was supplied by Britain. This impressive view shows a coach being loaded aboard ship at Dunkirk, destined for Alexandria. Four locomotives, possibly Class 545 2-6-0s, are visible behind. First-class coach No. 155 was one of twenty built in 1928 by Groupe Française. More were built by Leeds Forge, Metropolitan of Birmingham and Ringhoffer of Kopřivnice in what is now the Czech Republic. (Alon Siton Collection)

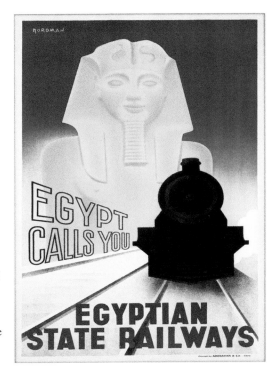

'Egypt Calls You' is another beautiful Egyptian State Railways poster from the golden age of rail travel. Dating from 1930, its design epitomises art deco, which was the prevalent iconic style of publicity material of that era. An ancient golden pharaoh smiles over a powerful steam locomotive and radiating rails in an attractive, perspective composition. (Alon Siton Collection)

Another panoramic, but undated, view over a tranquil Suez Canal zone with an assortment of four and six-wheeled goods wagons, and some ancient passenger coaches in sidings. The mosque in the centre appears to be the same building featured in the 1875 Zangaki Brothers image, but from a different viewpoint. The great waterway is visible in the background. (Alon Siton Collection)

This is a 1933 photograph of Kantara East station, where passengers on Palestine Railways' British-built Haifa to Cairo railway line crossed the Suez Canal on their long journey across the Sinai desert. To the left is the Customs House, and to the right a sign promises trains for Palestine, Syria, Transjordan and Iraq. Below it, another advertises sleeping cars to Cairo and, rather optimistically, for Calais and London! The line here was abandoned around seventy years ago, and no trains arrive here anymore. (Alon Siton Collection)

This vintage photograph shows the exterior of Luxor railway station sometime before the Second World War. Note the separate booking offices for first-, second- and third-class passengers, as well as the telegraph office to the left. Passenger trains arriving from Port Said and Cairo stopped here so that tourists could explore the famous temples along the Nile. (Alon Siton Collection)

The fifteen members of this class of outside-cylindered 2-4-2Ts dated from 1936. They were manufactured for Egyptian State Railways by William Bagnall & Co. of Stafford. This is the official workshop portrait of No. 1138. Some of them were still being used on sugar-cane traffic in the 1970s. (Alon Siton Collection)

By 1940, North Africa was in the throes of the Second World War. This fascinating photograph from that year shows Allied soldiers about to board a twin Sentinel steam railcar for Cairo, at Maadi station. Note the very British-looking signal box by the level crossing. (Alon Siton Collection)

Part of the Allied force in North Africa was the 25th New Zealand Battalion. Some of its men are seen here with a railcar consisting of two converted trucks, fitted with flanged wheels, patrolling the line to Matruh, west of Alexandria, during the first Libyan Campaign in 1941. (Alexander Turnbull Library, New Zealand)

Not all members of the armed forces were engaged in front line duty. Many were deployed on infrastructure, and the building of railways was vital for the transport of supplies. New Zealand's wartime Prime Minister, Peter Fraser, meets some of the personnel of a Railway Construction Unit in Egypt in May 1941. (Alexander Turnbull Library, New Zealand)

The Sunderland-built merchant ship SS *Thistlegorm* was only a year old when she set sail with a cargo including two Stanier 8F 2-8-0s bound for Alexandria, routed via the Cape of Good Hope. Having reached the north end of the Red Sea where it narrows into the Gulf of Suez, on 6 October 1941, she was sunk by Heinkel HE111s of the Luftwaffe, with the loss of nine of her crew. The sunken vessel and locomotives now form a popular scuba diving site. (João Pedro Silva)

A fine portrait of a crew of operatives of the New Zealand Railway Operating Unit taking a breather in Egypt's Western Desert on 12 December 1941. They appear to be posing on the running plate of one of the Class 545 2-6-0s, which is coupled to a brake van. (Alexander Turnbull Library, New Zealand)

One of the elegant 'Atlantics' simmers under the vast roof of Cairo Central. It was described as one of the world's busiest stations, a crossroads of the world to rival New York's Times Square. This would have been especially true when this photograph was taken in November 1942 as Allied troops of Britain, Ireland, Australia, New Zealand, South Africa, India and the rest passed through on their way to and from the desert front. (Alon Siton Collection)

Possibly taken somewhere near El Alamein, in the western desert, another Stanier 8F of the War Department, minus her tender, awaits attention. A United States Army Transportation Corps (USATC) Class S100 0-6-0T stands in the background. Several of these found their way to the Southern Railway in Britain after the war, becoming the 'USA' Class. (Alon Siton Collection)

As well as the S100 0-6-0Ts, the USA supplied Whitcomb diesel locomotives, which played an important role in North Africa. Steam locomotives in the desert were an easy target for the Luftwaffe. The diesels, though, were smokeless and easier to camouflage. One is seen here hauling an ambulance train in Egypt, crewed by engineers of the New Zealand Railway Operations Company, on 8 March 1943. (Alexander Turnbull Library, New Zealand)

This historic photograph shows the first train to arrive at El Alamein station following the Allies' decisive breakthrough in October 1942. The locomotive is being driven by a crew of New Zealand Army Engineers, who are replenishing water supplies. Note the rudimentary armour plating built around the footplate of the Stanier 8F. (Alexander Turnbull Library, New Zealand)

Ingenious solutions were improvised in wartime conditions. Here we have some British soldiers in Egypt preparing to operate quadruple Browning guns, which have been mounted on a rotating turret set in the roof of a converted goods van. (Alexander Turnbull Library, New Zealand)

Another Egyptian locomotive built by North British of Glasgow was 2-6-2T No. 1230 of 1926. Here she is with a Cairo to Helwan local train in the 1940s. She was part of a batch that was a continuation of a class built by Breda in Italy, with 5 feet 6.75 inch coupled wheels, the tank engine version of the more numerous Class 545 2-6-0. (Israel Railways Museum)

Another Bagnall product destined for Egypt was this 750 mm gauge 2-8-2, No. 2004, works No. 2889, of 1947. She was one of a pair built for the Western Oases Railway. Note the skirts covering her motion, presumably to prevent a build-up of desert sand on moving parts. (Alon Siton Collection)

Like many post-war nations, Egypt began to modernise the railway network that had suffered so much during the conflict. In 1948, Egyptian State Railways ordered twelve 1,600 hp diesel-electric locomotives from English Electric's Vulcan Foundry in Newton-le-Willows. They featured the unusual wheel arrangement of 1A-Do-A1 and were numbered 3001–3012. (Alon Siton Collection)

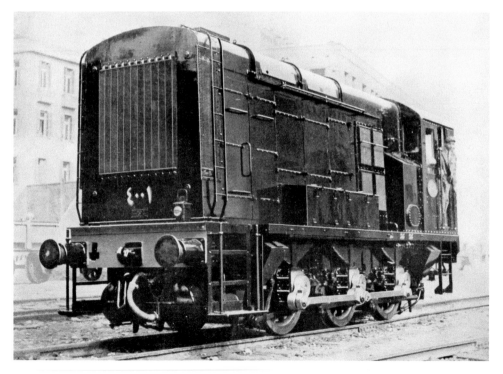

The big diesels seen above were not a great success, unlike this other product of English Electric, dating from the same year. No. 4001, seen here, was the first of fifteen 350 hp diesel-electric shunters built for Egypt, and they were joined later by eight more via the War Department. (Alon Siton Collection)

Continuing the English Electric diesel theme, in 1950 the company built these stylish multiple units for Egypt, with EE equipment installed in superstructure built by the Birmingham Railway Carriage & Wagon Co. Ten five-car sets were built for Cairo–Alexandria expresses along with another nine for suburban services. (Alon Siton Collection)

Alongside its new line of diesel locomotives, Vulcan Foundry continued to outshop steam traction into the post-war era. This is Egyptian State Railways 2-8-0 No. 760, works No. 6145, of 1951 awaiting shipment at Gladstone Dock, Liverpool, on 10 May 1952. Many examples of this new standard design were built by Vulcan Foundry as well as Henschel in Germany. (Alon Siton Collection)

This evocative Egyptian scene, possibly dating from the 1950s, harks back to a lost era. A 2-6-2T hauls a short passenger train against a backdrop of low hills. Some local people and their donkey walk along between a plantation and an irrigation canal. (Alon Siton Collection)

Resembling an exercise in perspective drawing, this photograph, also thought to date from the 1950s, shows an Egyptian State Railways passenger train hauled by another 2-6-2T. It is running parallel to road and canal traffic on the route between Port Said and Suez. (Alon Siton Collection)

In 1956, an attempt to regain control of the Suez Canal led to eastern Egypt being invaded by Israel, supported by Britain and France. Following the intervention of the United Nations, the invading powers withdrew. This photograph shows Egyptian State Railways Class G8 General Motors diesel No. 3519, carrying the UN flag, being waved through by British paratroopers as a UN Police Force made up of Norwegians arrive at El Cap, the British front line, en route from Abu Suweir to Port Said. (Alon Siton Collection)

It took eleven years to construct the Aswan Dam across the Nile, and it was completed in 1970. On 17 May 1964 a crowded train brings one of the three daily shifts of construction workers from the city of Aswan, half an hour away. (Alon Siton Collection)

A spectacular bird's-eye view of Cairo's elegant Ramses railway station in the 1960s. The handsome edifice was built in 1925, with a Moorish architectural motif adorning its northern and southern entrances. (Alon Siton Collection)

El Arish station was in northern Sinai on the British-built route between Haifa and Cairo. This view was taken in 1967, immediately after the Israeli takeover of the area in the Six Days War. 1956-built General Motors Class G8 diesel No. 3526 occupies the main line, still in original ESR colours. Beyond it are two other diesels in grey livery, and a steam crane can be seen on the right. This whole line was eventually abandoned and dismantled. (Israel Railway Museum)

Back in the Suez Canal zone in April 1969, this is the Firdan swing bridge that carried the railway over the northern narrows of the canal between Kantara and Ismailia. At this time it was officially neutral territory, with its own United Nations observation post in the foreground. There was a succession of railway bridges at this point, each with its own turbulent history. No trains have passed since the Six Day War of 1967, and the desert sands have covered the rails in this view, as the bridge stands open for Suez shipping. (Alon Siton Collection)

This is modern-looking Luxor station, probably in the 1980s, with two vintage British-built former royal saloons on the right. The clerestory-roofed vehicle was part of a private train built for the Khedive of Egypt in 1909/10 by Ashbury Works of Manchester. Behind it is an elliptical-roofed coach from King Fuad's Royal Train, delivered in 1924 by Metropolitan Carriage of Saltley, Birmingham. (Alon Siton Collection)

Sudan

The Station Khartoum - North

As in Egypt, tourist traffic was also encouraged south of the border in Sudan. This is Khartoum North station with Sudan Government Railways 4-4-0 locomotive No. 38, built by Baldwin in 1898. A member of her crew is performing one final inspection and lubrication prior to departure from the capital with a tourist train on the long journey through the desert to Port Sudan. (Alon Siton Collection)

A beautifully simple travel poster to tempt Europeans to sample the mysteries of the desert and the River Nile. Wadi Halfa, close to the Egyptian border, became a destination in the nineteenth century. The permanent railway here had its roots in the military campaigns of Kitchener, finally reaching the capital, Khartoum, in 1899. (Alon Siton Collection)

The steamboats on the Blue Nile, as seen in this vintage colourised postcard, were also operated by Sudan Government Railways. Such boats were used regularly to carry local passengers and tourists up and down the meandering river from Wadi Halfa to Aswan. (Alon Siton Collection)

Another vintage postcard, this one issued by G. N. Morhig, the English Pharmacy, Khartoum. It shows a panoramic view of Port Sudan station with a Sudan Government Railways passenger train, guarded by some magnificent semaphore signals. This Red Sea port was the embarkation point for many European and American tourists returning home by ship after exploring Sudan and Egypt. (Alon Siton Collection)

Hunslet & Co. of Leeds was best known for simple, dependable industrial locomotives for the domestic market. They also produced more complex machines for export, such as this outside-cylindered Sudan Government Railways 4-6-0T No. 17, built in 1897. (Alon Siton Collection)

Sudan Government Railways 4-6-0 No. 85 *Dakhla* was a product of the North British Locomotive Co., Glasgow, works No. 16754, of 1905. Her large cab and bogie tender were modern features for the time. (ETH Zürich)

As well as 4-6-0s, Sudan Government Railways employed locomotives of the 4-4-2 wheel arrangement. Four were built by Robert Stephenson & Co. in Darlington, in 1910, numbered 110–113. This is No. 112 at the head of the Wadi Halfa to Khartoum express. (Alon Siton Collection)

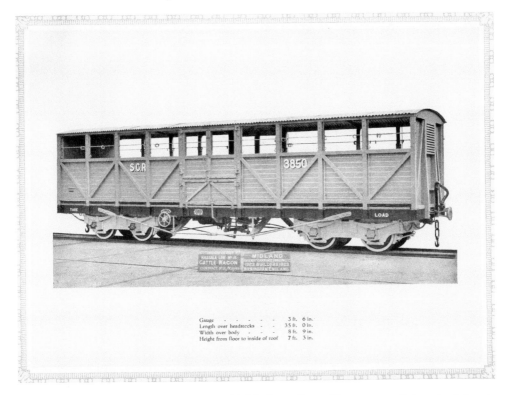

British industry also supplied goods vehicles to Middle East railways. They were usually bespoke designs to local specifications, such as this bogie livestock wagon, built by the Midland Railway Carriage & Wagon Co. in Birmingham. Interestingly, one of the boards in front reads 'Egyptian & Sudan Government Railways' suggesting joint operation. (Alon Siton Collection)

In December 1930, Wadi Halfa station is the setting for this Sudan Government Railways 4-6-2 on the Khartoum passenger train. This handsome 'Pacific' was possibly another locomotive built by North British of Glasgow. Note the coaching stock shaded against the fierce desert sun. (Alon Siton Collection)

Of very similar design to contemporary diesel-electric shunters for British railways, this is Sudan Government Railways No. 2, built by Hawthorn, Leslie of Newcastle in 1936, with a dependable 350 hp English Electric power unit. (ETH Zürich)

Looking immaculate outside a locomotive shed, Sudan Government Railways 4-6-2 No. 2804 awaits her next duty. She was built by North British Locomotive Co. of Glasgow for the War Department in 1942. (Alon Siton Collection)

Another NBL 'Pacific', WD No. 2815 heads the Khartoum train at Wadi Halfa in 1944. The Nile Valley route between the Egyptian and Sudanese capitals involved two transhipments. The 550 miles from Cairo to Shellal, south of Aswan, was covered by an Egyptian State Railways train. A Sudanese steamer then carried the passengers along 210 miles of the Nile to Wadi Halfa. The remaining 574 miles to Khartoum was on the Sudan rail network. (Alon Siton Collection)

This is the magnificent sight of brand-new Co-Co diesel-electric No. 1024 inside Vulcan Foundry in 1961. She was one of fifty-five such 1,875 hp locomotives built for Sudan by English Electric, with that distinctive EE nose end. Incidentally the electric locomotive in the background was destined for Poland, illustrating the diversity of Vulcan Foundry's output. (Alon Siton Collection)

Iraq

A freight train hauled by an ex-Indian metre gauge 4-6-0 crosses the Euphrates. This is the bridge at Al-Qurnah in southern Iraq, around 74 km north-west of Basra, at the confluence of the Tigris and Euphrates where they form the Shatt al-Arab. In local folklore it is the site of the Garden of Eden. (Alon Siton Collection)

The crew of Iraqi State Railways Class HGS No. 151 pose with their charge at the head of a passenger train composed of characteristic Iraqi coaching stock. The 4-6-0 was built by Vulcan Foundry at Newton-le-Willows in 1920. (Eldorado postcard, Alon Siton Collection)

An interesting bilingual sign, in English and Arabic, at Baghdad West station, proudly (and slightly inaccurately) proclaiming 'Iraqi State Railways – Baghdad West standard gauge station for Samarrah, Baiji, Mosul, Aleppo, Ankara, Istanbul, Paris and London'. (Alon Siton Collection)

Probably the most glamorous locomotive type to operate in the Middle East was Iraqi State Railways' streamlined PC Class 4-6-2. No doubt influenced by Gresley's A4s and Stanier's 'Coronations', four were built by Robert Stephenson Hawthorn of Darlington in 1940, although one was lost at sea. This is No. 502 *Mosul* at her namesake station on 17 February 1943. (Alon Siton Collection)

Another American S100 0-6-0T, this time in the ownership of Iraqi State Railways and numbered 1212. She had previously been War Department No. 1292 and was built by Davenport in Iowa as works No. 2422 of 1942. (Alon Siton Collection)

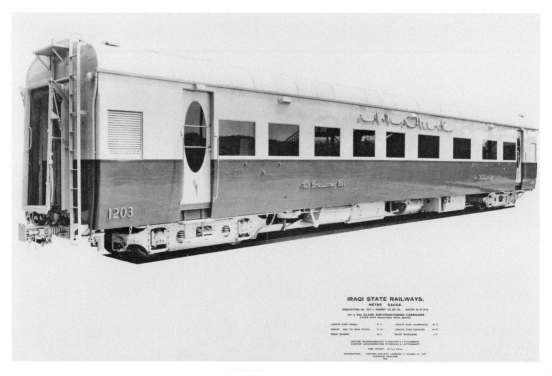

An elegant First-class air-conditioned coach for Iraq's metre gauge railway system, built by the Cravens Railway Carriage & Wagon Co. of Sheffield, England, in 1952. This is Iraqi State Railways No. 1203 in an official works portrait. Note the beautiful raised lettering on the bodyside. (Alon Siton Collection)

An American 'Austerity' (MacArthur) 2-8-2 of Iraqi State Railways approaches Baghdad with a train from Basra in 1953. Note the locals wandering freely on the permanent way and the British-style mechanical signalling. (Alon Siton Collection)

So successful was the Stanier 8F 2-8-0 at home and abroad that many post-Second World War locomotive orders for Egypt and Iraq were based on its design, although with some modifications. German companies Henschel and Krupp, as well as Hungary's Mavag, all built 8F 'lookalikes' for Egypt and Iraq. This is Krupp 2-8-0 No. 1446 in service in Iraq, seen in 1956. (Alon Siton Collection)

Iraqi State Railways 2-6-2T No. 326, seen here at Baghdad in 1957, was built by Hawthorn Leslie in Newcastle as works No. 3151 of 1916. She was originally ordered for the Assam Bengal Railway but was initially sent to east Africa, then to Iraq around 1919. (Alon Siton Collection)

Another Leeds manufacturer known mostly for British industrial locomotives was Hudswell Clarke. They were the builders of this modern 2-8-4T for the Iraq Petroleum Company, No. 2, works No. 1853, of 1951, seen here at Kirkuk in 1967. (Alon Siton Collection)

More Iraqi locomotive variety as Class Z 2-8-2 No. 96 pauses at Basra on 15 March 1967. She was built by Maschinenfabrik Esslingen of Mettingen, Germany, as works No. 5194 of 1956. (Alon Siton Collection)

Iraqi State Railways No. 193 was formerly South Indian Railway Class HGS 4-6-0 No. 116. She was built by North British in Glasgow as works No. 23034 of 1923. She was shipped to Iraq by the War Department during the Second World War and is seen here at Baghdad East with a passenger train in 1967. (Alon Siton Collection)

An American import at work on Iraqi State Railways, Class W 2-8-2 No. 64, at Baghdad on 17 March 1967. She was previously USATC Class S200 No. 73060, built by Alco of Schenectady, New York, as works No. 71040 of 1943. (Alon Siton Collection)

Another former Indian metre gauge 4-6-0, this time running tender-first, Iraqi State Railways No. 144. She was built for the Madras & Southern Mahratta Railway as their No. 180 by Nasmyth, Wilson of Manchester, works No. 896 of 1909. She was sent to Iraq in 1917 and is seen here at Kirkuk on 19 March 1967. (Alon Siton Collection)

Jordan

A fascinating view of the Hedjaz Railway's main line and railway bridge in Naharayim, in the northern Jordan Valley. Naharayim means 'two rivers' in Hebrew, being the confluence of the Jordan and the Yarmuk. The Hedjaz Railway's main line from Haifa to Dera'a Junction, in Syria, crossed the Yarmuk here. Sadly, the bridge was destroyed and the train service to Syria ended. (Israel Railways Museum)

The first and largest girder bridge across the Yarmuk Creek, on the Hedjaz route between Haifa and Dera'a, in 1908. A tank locomotive with a solitary flat wagon is seen crossing the river. Colonel T. E. Lawrence tried to destroy this bridge during his first ride through Syria in June 1917. (J. H. Halladjian, Alon Siton Collection)

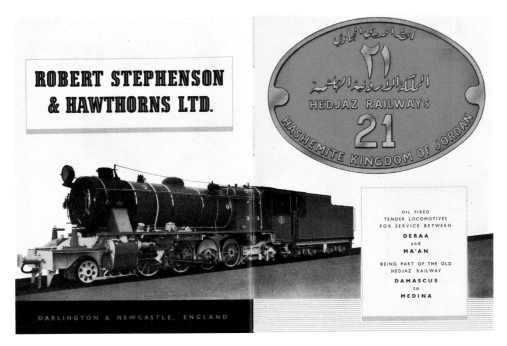

The period immediately after the Second World War was a boom time for British locomotive manufacturers as the world re-equipped its railways. Hedjaz Railway No. 21 was one of three handsome 2-8-2s built by Robert Stephenson & Hawthorn in Darlington. The trio carried works Nos 7431–7433 of 1952. (Robert Stephenson & Hawthorn catalogue, Alon Siton Collection)

Photographed in 1980 at the main station in Jordan's capital, Amman, is Hedjaz Railway No. 23, RSH No. 7433 of 1952. Note the single central buffer and cowcatcher on an otherwise very British-looking locomotive. Remarkably, she survives in operation today. (Alon Siton Collection)

An example of an early Japanese export: Hedjaz Railway's 4-6-2 No. 82 was built at Nippon Sharyo Locomotive Works, their No. 1610 of 1959. She is seen here at the Jordanian border with Syria in 1986. (Alon Siton Collection)

As the twentieth century came to a close, steam was still hard at work on the remaining section of the Hedjaz Jordan Railway. Here, 2-8-2 No. 51, built by Arnold Jung of Kirchen, Germany, works No. 12081 of 1955, heads a freight train near Amman in 1997. (Alon Siton Collection)

The same photographer at the same location was rewarded with the sight of a short passenger train hauled by No. 61, a brutish-looking 2-6-2T built by Haine St Pierre in Belgium, works No. 2147 of 1955. (Alon Siton Collection)

Turkey

Neilson's of Glasgow was one of the three constituent companies that amalgamated to form the great North British Locomotive Co., along with Dübs and Sharp Stewart. All three companies enjoyed an international reputation and this official photo shows a handsome 4-4-0 built for the Ottoman Railway Co., works No. 4247 of 1890. (ETH Zürich)

Despite coming from a different manufacturer, this classic British outline 0-6-0, also destined for the Ottoman Railway, bears a strong family resemblance to the 4-4-0 above. She was built by Robert Stephenson & Co. in Darlington as works No. 3422 of 1911, and eventually became Turkish State Railways (TCDD) No. 33.021. (Alon Siton Collection)

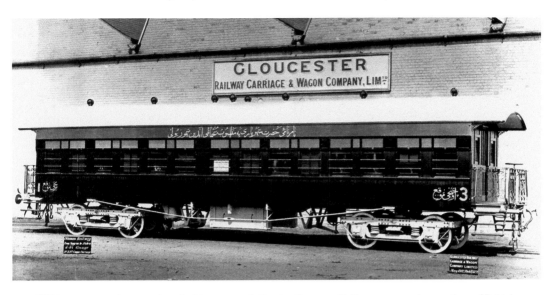

With open verandas at each end, this new coach for the Ottoman Railway was another product of British industry. She is posed for her official works photograph outside the Gloucester Railway Carriage & Wagon Co. (Alon Siton Collection)

This is TCDD No. 46104, formerly Ottoman Railway No. 133. She was one of six powerful 2-8-2s supplied by Robert Stephenson & Co. as works No. 3996 of 1929, and is pictured here at Izmir Basmane station. Sister locomotive No. 46103 is preserved at the railway museum at Çamlik. (Alon Siton Collection)

A particularly difficult section of the Ottoman Railway from Smyrna to Egherdir included gradients of 1 in 36 over the Azizieh Pass. This impressive Beyer Garratt 2-8-0+0-8-2 articulated locomotive was ordered from Beyer Peacock of Gorton in 1927, works No. 6324. (Alon Siton collection)

TCDD 4-6-4T No. 3078, built in 1925, heads a lengthy passenger train near Istanbul. Eight of these engines were ordered from Henschel by the CFOA (Chemins de fer Ottomans d'Anatolie) but delivered to TCDD. They were in use on commuter trains until electrification in the 1970s. (Alon Siton Collection)

TCDD 2-10-0 No. 56140, seen at Ankara in 1970, was one of a batch of fifty such locomotives built by Škoda in Czechoslovakia in 1949 to a German Reichsbahn design. Others of the same class were built in Britain by Vulcan Foundry in 1939, although the war delayed their delivery until the late 1940s. (Alon Siton Collection)

This is veteran TCDD Class G8 0-8-0 No. 44064 in 1972. The eighty-three members of the class were of German origin and arrived in Turkey by various means. Some came from France, taken as reparation after the First World War. Others were simply supplied by the Germans to the Ottoman Empire. At least two are preserved in Turkey and a third engine survives in Germany. (Alon Siton Collection)

Three of these long, centre-cab, diesel-hydraulic locomotives were built in Germany by Krauss Maffei for TCDD, gaining the nickname 'Turkish Crocodiles'. They were a six-axle centre-cab version of the German V200, with twin Maybach engines and Voith transmission. The crew of No. 27003 pose as their charge heads a freight train. (Alon Siton Collection)

More German influence in Turkey as a TCDD 1951-built Class MT5300 DMU passes Dursunbey in 1977. The sixteen three-car units were descended from the legendary pre-war Fliegende Hamburger unit and built by MAN/Esslingen. Originally intended for long-distance travel, they had dining and bar facilities. (Alon Siton Collection)

Lebanon

The French influence in Lebanon is clear to see in the architecture of Beirut station in this charming view of 1895. This was the original departure point on the 1,050 mm gauge line to Damascus. (Alon Siton Collection)

This 1895 view of a newly completed embankment and cutting gives some idea of the terrain the engineers conquered as the line climbed out of Beirut on its way to the Syrian capital. An engineers' train can be discerned beyond the cutting. (Alon Siton Collection)

Around 3 miles east of Beirut the line passed Jamhour, and here the same little engineers' train appears in a view that clearly shows the toothed rack rail between the running rails. (Alon Siton Collection)

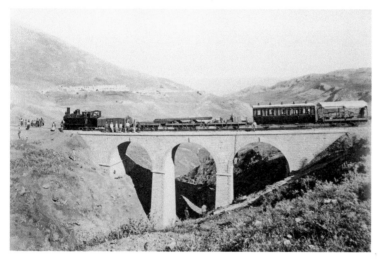

The beautiful three-arched viaduct at Khan Mourad was destroyed in the Lebanese civil war, and today motorway traffic speeds past. That little engineers' train makes another appearance in this 1895 photograph. (Alon Siton Collection)

The Haifa, Beirut & Tripoli Railway was, for a short time, the main railway along the Lebanese coastline. The line tunnelled through the chalk headland at Rosh Hanikra (Ras Naqura). This Robinson Class 8K 2-8-0 is emerging on the Lebanese side of the tunnels in the 1940s with a short train consisting of a four-wheeled auxiliary water tank and a USATC brake van. (Alon Siton Collection)

The HB&TR was inaugurated in 1942 as a military extension of the British-built line from Cairo to Haifa. Having operated for only five years, plans to continue the line northwards via western Syria into Turkey were abandoned owing to the political conflict in the Middle East. The entire route was abandoned in 1947, two years after this photograph was taken of the blockhouse at Jbeil. (Alon Siton Collection)

Beirut shed in 1968, housing three locomotives of the Chemin de fer de l'État Libanais. All were built in Switzerland by Schweizerische Lokomotiv und Maschinenfabrik of Winterthur, and are, from left to right, a Class S 0-10-0T, a Class B 0-6-2T and a Class A 0-8-2T. (Alon Siton Collection)

A rare 1968 photograph taken somewhere in the Lebanese highlands between Beirut and Damascus in Syria. The locomotive is one of seven Swiss Class A 0-8-2Ts, built by SLM in 1906. The line closed in 1976 at the time of the civil war. (Alon Siton Collection)

Syria

This charming vintage postcard shows the Hedjaz Railway's Kanawat terminus in Damascus before the First World War. This was the starting point for passenger trains to Jordan and Arabia, but only from 1908 to 1920. It still stands today, a reminder of bygone times in Syria, although trains no longer depart from here. (Alon Siton Collection)

A rare view of a train crossing the Orontes River in Syria in 1925. Note, on the left, the remains of the previous girder bridge, presumably destroyed by T. E. Lawrence. The locomotive is a DHP Class G 0-8-0T, built in 1906 by Société Française de Constructions Mécaniques. The train consists of a four-wheel coach built by Franco-Belge and a former Wagons-Lits dining car built by Ringhoffer in 1912 and sent to Palestine in 1922. (Alon Siton Collection)

Another striking travel poster from the heyday of the steam railway, this time by the Chemins de fer de Paris à Lyon et à la Méditerranée, exhorts travellers to 'Visit Syria & Lebanon by train'. Note that the railway company has addresses in Paris and Cairo. (Alon Siton Collection)

A stark reminder that the glory days of railway tourism in the Middle East were cruelly cut short by conflict, this rail-borne Turkish armoured car is seen in Syria. Note the '*Hicaz Demiryolu*' (Hedjaz Railway) inscription on the plating. (Mitchell Library, New South Wales)

Watched by an armed soldier, the Baghdad Express draws into Meidan Ekbis station on the border between Turkey and Syria on 9 July 1942. The locomotive is Prussian-built Class G10 2-8-2 No. 901, formerly of the Société Ottomane du Chemin de fer Damas-Hama et prolongements, known as DHP. (M. D. Elias, Alexander Turnbull Library, New Zealand)

New Zealand Engineers unloading a Robinson Class 8K 2-8-0 at a Syrian port on 22 May 1942. This type of locomotive was used extensively overseas by the Railway Operating Department in the First World War and the War Department in the Second World War. (H. Paton, Alexander Turnbull Library, New Zealand)

We are used to seeing archive images of women taking on all kinds of roles during wartime. It was unusual, however, to see women employed in ballast laying, as is the case with these Syrians under the direction of the New Zealand Railway Construction Company on 15 September 1942. (M. D. Elias, Alexander Turnbull Library, New Zealand)

A nostalgic view of two vintage Hedjaz Railway four-wheeled coaches, Nos 359 and 363, at the terminus at Damascus in 1965. Note the elaborate ventilation arrangements above the windows and within the roof of each vehicle. (Alon Siton Collection)

Also at Damascus in the same year, in contrast with the wooden-bodied coaches above, this photograph shows Hedjaz Railway 2-8-2 No. 259, built by Hartmann of Chemnitz, Germany, in 1918, works No. 4028. (Alon Siton Collection)

The Syrian town of Dera'a is just over the border from Jordan and was the first terminus of the Hedjaz Railway in that country. De Dion-Bouton petrol railcar No. ACM3 of 1930 is seen here in 2008. Note the four-wheeled bogie at the front and single driven axle at the rear. (Jan Hajek, Alon Siton Collection)

Cadem station, on the outskirts of Damascus, was the location of the main Hedjaz Railway workshops in Syria. Today, surviving steam locomotives are being restored by enthusiasts. In May 2008, Hartmann 2-8-2 No. 262, works No. 4031 of 1918, is undergoing maintenance. (Jan Hajek, Alon Siton Collection)

Another 2008 view of the facility at Cadem with a bogie luggage van on the left, some passenger stock on the right, and, in the centre, what appears to be a 2-8-0 with her smokebox door open. (Jan Hajek, Alon Siton collection)

2008 scenes showing Aleppo's historic railway station and a close-up of its old Baghdad Railway bell. (Alon Siton Collection)

Iran

An interesting wartime photograph taken by an American stationed in Iran. It shows the aftermath of a head-on collision, presumably at slow speed, somewhere on a remote mountainous stretch of the Trans-Iranian Railway in 1942. (Alon Siton Collection)

Back on the rails, this photograph taken from a train window gives an impression of the dramatic mountain scenery traversed by the Trans-Iranian Railway in the 1940s. (Alon Siton Collection)

Even more spectacular is this original 'Irantour' postcard showing a train crossing the Veresk bridge, east of Tehran. The locomotive is one of a class of four Garratt 2-8-4+4-8-2s built by Beyer Peacock at the Gorton Foundry in 1936. Before the Allied invasion of 1941, they were the only British-built standard gauge locomotives in Iran. (Alon Siton Collection)

This diminutive 2-foot 6-inch gauge oil-fired 0-6-2T was built by William Bagnall of Stafford for the Anglo-Iranian Oil Company immediately after the Second World War. (Alon Siton Collection)

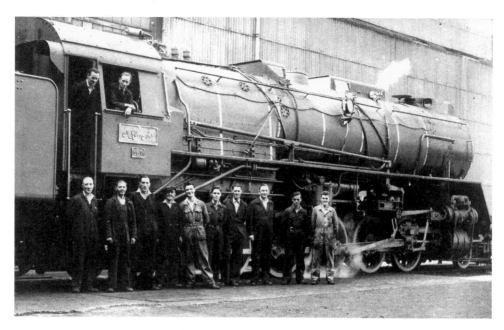

Sixty-four of these massive, oil-fired 2-10-2s were ordered from Vulcan Foundry by the Iranian State Railway from 1952. They were of modern design, being fitted with roller bearings, air brakes and electric lighting. In Iran they were known as Class 52 and at least one is thought to survive at the new Mashhad Railway Museum. (Alon Siton Collection)

Like most of the world's railways from the 1950s onwards, Iran stopped importing locomotives from Britain and turned to the USA. General Motors/EMD is a major player in the international market and in 1978 one of its products, a Class G12 Bo-Bo, is seen at work in Iran. (Alon Siton Collection)